GUIDE TO MODIFIED EXHAUST SYSTEMS

A Reference for Law Enforcement Officers and Motor Vehicle Inspectors

Noise Free America: A Coalition to Promote Quiet

Fresno, Californ

T0122658

Guide to Modified Exhaust Systems
A Reference for Law Enforcement Officers
and Motor Vehicle Inspectors

Published by Quill Driver Books
An imprint of Linden Publishing
2006 South Mary Street, Fresno, California 93721
(559) 233-6633 / (800) 345-4447
QuillDriverBooks.com

Quill Driver Books and Colophon are trademarks of
Linden Publishing, Inc.

ISBN 978-1-61035-312-0

135798642

Printed in the United States of America
on acid-free paper.

Library of Congress Cataloging-in-Publication Data on file.

Contents

Foreword

During my 31-year career with the Houston Police Department, my most challenging responsibility was enforcing laws relevant to vehicular noise. When I began my noise enforcement initiative, I was unprepared for the anger, animosity, and hatred I would incur from motorcycle organizations whose members and leadership considered themselves to be above the law and "entitled" as they regularly assaulted the motoring and pedestrian public with decibel levels two to four times the safe limit, as mandated by the Environmental Protection Agency.

Illegal vehicular noise is a growing national problem, due to the lack of effective enforcement. Vehicular noise enforcement, to be effective, must be proactive in nature, not reactive. The general public, having been victimized by illegal vehicular noise for many decades, erroneously believes that certain motor vehicles (especially motorcycles) are designed to be loud. This false perception is reinforced by the obvious lack of enforcement on the part of local and state law enforcement officials. I am fully aware of the legal and logistical challenges inherent in undertaking a proactive law enforcement initiative relevant to illegal vehicular noise enforcement, but those who willingly and knowingly assault the general public via the operation of illegally loud motor vehicles must be brought under control.

I have personally reviewed this guide and find the pictorial section and associated text to be an excellent reference for any enforcement officer endeavoring to enforce vehicular noise laws. "To Protect and Serve" should be more than a placard on the side of a patrol vehicle, and the general public deserves to be protected from those who knowingly and willingly deny them the right to enjoy domestic tranquility and an environment free from excessive, intrusive, and dangerous illegal noise.

—Ricky Holtsclaw, Houston Police Department, retired

Introduction

Excessive noise is a serious threat to public health. High noise levels are associated with sleep deprivation, hearing loss, heart disease, chronic fatigue, aggressive behavior, and ringing of the ears. Excessive noise denies individuals the right to peacefully enjoy their own home and property.

Noise damages communities and reduces property values. The Census Bureau reports that noise is Americans' #1 complaint about their neighborhood and the #1 reason they wish to move. Excessive noise degrades the quality of life for millions of Americans. Law enforcement officials should not only be protecting public safety; they should also be protecting the public's health and well being.

This guide concerns excessive noise that is caused by the illegal tampering of a vehicle's exhaust system. By definition, a modified exhaust is not of the type installed at the time of manufacture, does not meet the manufacturer's specifications, and does not comply with manufacturing regulatory standards. This includes noise emissions. This practice results in a modified exhaust system. Motorcycles outfitted with modified exhaust systems (especially those made by Harley-Davidson) are the rule rather than the exception. In addition, modified exhaust systems on cars and light trucks are becoming increasingly popular.

Beginning in 1983, the EPA issued regulations requiring all motorcycles destined for the American market to be equipped with certified mufflers that maintain motorcycle total noise emissions to no more than 83 dBA for motorcycles manufactured from January 1, 1983, to December 31, 1985, and no more than 80 dBA for motorcycles manufactured after January 1, 1986. The regulations also require that the motorcycle mufflers be labeled to certify compliance. In this guide, those mufflers are referred to as "EPA-compliant" mufflers.

This guide proposes a new approach to enforcing state statutes and local ordinances that prohibit the use of modified exhaust systems on motor vehicles. For motorcycles, we propose a new paradigm in which law enforcement shifts attention to the root *cause* of the problem—the modified exhaust system—and away from the *symptoms* of the problem, the offending excessive and unusual noise. This shift of thinking leads to a very officer-friendly method with which to effectively address this problem.

The premise of this guide is that a very large percentage of the modified exhaust systems in use today are readily recognizable by sight alone, and often at considerable distance. The officer's observation that the exhaust in question displays excessive and unusual noise will support their identification based on sight. Once the trained officer gets visual confirmation of the offending exhaust, no other requirements must be met to qualify for a well-deserved citation. Documenting the offending exhaust system with unequivocal photographic evidence will provide all the objective evidence needed for a citation to hold up in court.

For this new approach to work, the officer must first be able to recognize a modified exhaust system on sight. Fortunately, this is surprisingly easy in most cases. For those exhaust systems easiest to identify by sight alone, a few hours studying this guide will enable law enforcement officers to begin issuing citations with confidence.

For the small percentage of modified exhaust systems that do not permit rapid identification by sight alone, this guide offers additional guidance to more definitive measures that must be taken. However, enforcement based solely on sight alone should be sufficient to significantly reduce the problem. When that reduction has been achieved, time will become available to focus attention on the remaining offenders, with the aid of this guide.

Finally, in order for the information outlined in this guide to be of maximum benefit to law enforcement agencies, local or state laws should specifically prohibit the use of modified exhaust systems. Currently, there are at least 18 states that have done so. We at Noise Free America: A Coalition to Promote Quiet urge other states to follow suit by incorporating this concept into state law.

How to Identify Modified Exhaust Systems on Motorcycles by Physical Appearance

GENERAL FEATURES OF A PROPER MUFFLER

The information in this section is very basic; no real knowledge of the appearance of stock exhaust systems is required. We believe the average law enforcement officer or motor vehicle inspector can easily assimilate most of this information in a few hours.

There are only two broad categories of modified exhaust systems which will be presented in this section, yet they comprise as much as 60 to 70 percent of all modified exhaust systems. These two categories include the straight pipes and the after-market exhausts where the manufacturer proudly displays the company logo in a conspicuous location on the body of the muffler. These after-market manufacturer logos tell the world the exhaust system on this vehicle has been modified. Obviously, this information enables the officer to make a positive, unequivocal identification of the modified exhaust, often at considerable distance.

If law enforcement officers and motorcycle inspectors on a nation-wide basis addressed just these two categories of easily identified modified exhaust systems, the problem of excessive exhaust noise from motorcycles would be significantly reduced.

Before one can fully appreciate the look of straight pipes, one should first become familiar with the general appearance of a typical stock muffler. By definition, a proper muffler must have an expansion chamber. The expansion chamber contains the sound-deadening internal workings of the muffler, and will thus necessitate an increase in diameter near the end of the exhaust system.

However, a cautionary statement is in order. It is very important to understand the following concept: *All mufflers, by definition, will display an expansion chamber, but not all mufflers with an expansion chamber meet EPA standards, and will thus be regarded as examples of modified exhaust systems.* The overwhelming majority of after-market exhausts which fall into this category do not meet EPA regulations for noise emissions. We will address this category further in this section.

To get an appreciation for the appearance of an expansion chamber, consider the following ten examples of the EPA-compliant, stock exhaust systems which occur on the following motorcycles.

Figure 1. Harley-Davidson Softail stock exhaust displaying expansion chambers.

Figure 2. Suzuki Boulevard stock exhaust displaying expansion chambers.

Figure 3. Yamaha FZR 1000 EXUP stock exhaust
displaying expansion chamber.

Figure 4. BMW R1150R stock exhaust
displaying expansion chamber.

Figure 5. Honda VTX 1300C stock exhaust
displaying expansion chambers.

**Figure 6. Honda Shadow VLX stock exhaust
displaying expansion chambers.**

**Figure 7. Yamaha 650 V-Star stock exhaust
displaying expansion chambers.**

**Figure 8. Harley-Davidson Night Rod Special stock exhaust
displaying expansion chambers.**

Figure 9. Kawasaki Vulcan stock exhaust
displaying expansion chamber.

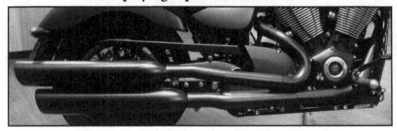

Figure 10. Victory Gunner stock exhaust
displaying expansion chambers.

How to Identify Straight Pipes

Straight pipes are the most egregious form of modified exhaust systems in use today. Straight pipes, also known as drag pipes, were never intended for use on public roadways. Like their name implies, drag pipes were designed for closed-course circuits only.

Straight pipes generally have absolutely no sound-deadening capabilities. Rather, they are merely hollow tubes. Very importantly, sound baffles are sometimes optional equipment for insertion into straight pipes, but the presence of sound baffles never constitutes an actual muffler. Hence, even with sound baffles installed, the exhaust system still falls short of being compliant with EPA guidelines, and would also thus qualify as a prime example of a modified exhaust system, as the noise emissions from straight pipes, with baffles installed, will exceed that of stock.

The hallmark appearance of straight pipes is the continuous diameter throughout the entire length of the exhaust system (including the exhaust headers). Generally, this diameter will range from 1 and 3/4 inches to 2 and 1/2 inches. The reason straight pipes never constitute a proper muffler, even when sound baffles are present, is because a true muffler will have an expansion chamber.

Figure 11. Harley-Davidson Softail with straight pipes.

Figure 12. Harley-Davidson Softail with straight pipes.

Figure 13. Harley-Davidson Sportster with straight pipes and heat tape.

Figure 14. Honda cruiser with Vance & Hines straight pipes.

**Figure 15. Victory motorcycle with straight pipes
wrapped in heat tape.**

It is important to realize that straight pipes are not always "straight" in physical appearance (as the ones pictured above). In fact, many straight pipes will contain conspicuous curved shapes. Again, these exhaust systems are merely hollow tubes without an expansion chamber, and they display the classic appearance of a continuous diameter throughout the entire exhaust system.

Figure 16. Custom-made chopper with
"curved" straight pipes.

Figure 17. Harley-Davidson Dyna with
"curved" straight pipes.

Figure 18. Custom-made chopper with "curved" straight pipes.

Figure 19. Harley-Davidson Dyna with "curved" straight pipes.

Figure 20. Close-up view of classic, "curved" straight pipes on a custom-made chopper.

An officer will encounter slight variations to the examples of straight pipes given above. There are a number of exhaust "end treatments" which may also be added to straight pipes like this "shark tail" end treatment pictured below. *Very importantly: end treatments do not constitute an expansion chamber.*

Figure 21. Custom-made chopper outfitted with straight pipes and shark tail-end treatment.

Figure 22. Yamaha Road Star with "curved" straight pipes.

Figure 23. Honda Shadow where owner has cut off both EPA-approved mufflers from a factory-installed exhaust system. This blatant example of illegal tampering approximates straight pipes.

STOCK EXHAUST POTENTIALLY CONFUSED WITH STRAIGHT PIPES

The presence of an expansion chamber separates stock mufflers from straight pipes. Pictured below are images of EPA-approved, stock exhaust systems where the expansion chamber is rather inconspicuous. Their appearance approaches that of a "continuous diameter," as seen with the classic appearance of straight pipes. However, the stock exhausts below either have a subtle constricting taper at the very end of the exhaust, or tapering where they start to merge with the exhaust headers. Straight pipes never display any tapering to the exhaust.

Perhaps easier to appreciate is the relatively "fat" appearance of these stock exhausts, as compared to the relatively "skinny" look of straight pipes. These two features should safely separate the straight pipes from those stock exhaust systems which do not display a prominent expansion chamber.

Figure 24. Indian Roadmaster with large diameter exhaust with slight taper at end of exhaust.

Figure 25. Honda Goldwing with large-diameter, stock exhaust, with a slight tapered effect at the end of the exhaust system.

AFTER-MARKET EXHAUSTS DISPLAYING COMPANY LOGOS

There is another broad category of modified exhaust systems which are very easy to recognize by sight alone. This is because many after-market companies prominently display their company logos on the body of the muffler.

Since it is exceedingly rare that any of these companies produce a product which is actually compliant with EPA regulations, one knows instantly if the exhaust system in question is illegal for use on a public roadway. Simple photographic documentation of the exhaust system displaying the company logo will provide sufficient, objective, verifiable evidence of the non-compliant exhaust. Some of these company logos are so conspicuous they could easily be spotted at a distance of 100 feet. This is especially true for the after-market exhausts companies catering to the sport bike industry.

The logos appearing on chrome exhausts are not very noticeable. This is true because the contrast of the wording is not particularly prominent with this "chrome on chrome" appearance. Nonetheless, the officer should pay close attention to spot these subtle logos, as they are virtually conclusive evidence the officer is dealing with a modified exhaust system. Motorcycles classified as cruisers are most likely to display this "chrome on chrome appearance." However, it is an entirely different situation with the sport bike industry, as they often go to the opposite extreme.

Some of the companies displaying company logos in a conspicuous location on cruisers include Vance & Hines, Rinehart Racing, Cobra, Python, SuperTrapp, Samson, Hooker, Caliber, BUB Enterprises, and Rush Exhaust.

As a leading producer of modified exhaust systems, the Vance & Hines logo is one of the most commonly seen logos the officer is likely to encounter. Below is a typical example of the Vance & Hines logo.

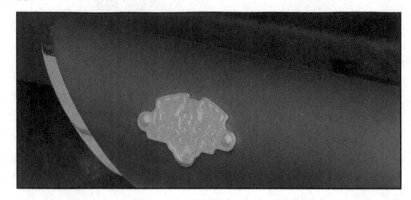

Figure 26. Vance & Hines logo on black pipes.

Figure 27. Crusher logo on Harley-Davidson
touring model.

Figure 28. Vance & Hines logo on chrome pipes.

Figure 29. RCX exhaust logo on chrome pipes.

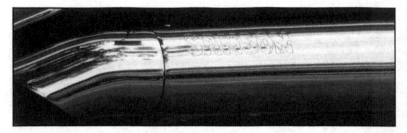

Figure 30. Samson logo on Harley-Davidson.

Figure 31. Vance & Hines logo on Honda cruiser.

Figure 32. Cobra Company logo on straight pipes.

Figure 33. Rinehart Racing company logo on
Harley-Davidson touring model.

Figure 34. Python Company logo on chrome pipes.

Figure 35. Hooker logo on chrome straight pipes.

Unlike many of the relatively subtle company logos found on the chrome pipes of the typical cruiser or touring motorcycle, company logos for the sport bike industry are often quite conspicuous. Knowing this, it will be apparent from a distance if one is dealing with an example of a modified exhaust system displaying one of these frequently gaudy logos. Only the Akrapovic and Yoshimura companies offer an EPA-compliant product (see page 57).

Figure 36. Akrapovic Company logo on BMW sport bike.

Figure 37. FMF company logo on Honda sport bike.

Figure 38. D&D company logo on sport bike.

Figure 39. Yoshimura company logo on sport bike.

Figure 40. Muzzy company logo on
Kawasaki ZRX 1200R sport bike.

Figure 41. Brock's company logo on Hayabusa sport bike.

Figure 42. Micron company logo on Suzuki
GSX 1300 sport bike.

Figure 43. M4 company logo on sport bike.

Figure 44. Two Brothers company logo
on Honda sport bike.

Figure 45. SC Project company logo on Ducati sport bike.

Figure 46. Termignoni company logo on Ducati sport bike.

Figure 47. Hindle company logo on sport bike.

Figure 48. Force Exhaust company logo on sport bike.

Figure 49. Jardine Exhaust company logo
on Honda sport bike.

Figure 50. HMF company logo on Yamaha sport bike.

2

Identifying Modified Exhaust Systems Where Knowledge of Factory-Installed Equipment Is Essential

This chapter will require familiarity with factory-installed exhaust systems in order to identify additional modified exhaust systems. This is true primarily because there are a fair number of after-market companies which do not put company logos on their products.

The best resource to view images of a wide variety of motorcycles in stock condition (many dating back to 2000) is TotalMotorcycle.com. From the home page, the officer or inspector is just three clicks away from viewing these images.

Some motorcycle manufacturers produce their own brand of after-market exhausts which are not EPA-compliant. These non-EPA approved exhausts *may* be featured in TotalMotorcycle.com.

Because Harley-Davidson motorcycles are the ones most frequently outfitted with modified exhaust systems, we have chosen to focus on this company's products to help law enforcement learn the features of their EPA-compliant, factory-installed exhaust systems. Once the officer has knowledge of the appearance of stock equipment, the non-compliant, after-market exhausts will become very apparent.

GENERAL FEATURES OF FACTORY-INSTALLED EXHAUST SYSTEMS ON HARLEY-DAVIDSON MOTORCYCLES

There are a couple of features of factory-installed exhaust systems on Harley-Davidson motorcycles which are important to learn.

Typically, the mufflers on all of their Sportsters, Dynas, Softails, and touring models are tapered at both ends. Pay particular attention to the tapered appearance at the end of the muffler. Below is the classic look to their tapered exhausts. *Conversely, non-EPA-compliant, after-market exhausts are almost never tapered at the end of the exhaust. This is a very important distinction.*

Figure 51. Classic tapered look to mufflers installed on Harley-Davidson Sportsters, Dynas, and Softails.

Figure 52. Although subtle, the tapering in the last few inches of this stock, Harley-Davidson muffler has been the classic look on their touring models for decades.

Some Harley-Davidson factory-installed exhausts do not show tapering at the end. Plus, Harley-Davidson's EPA-compliant Screamin' Eagle Exhausts also do not show tapering at the end, and thus resemble the non-compliant after-market exhausts. However, to separate Harley's own Screamin' Eagle exhausts from the non-EPA-compliant exhausts, the conspicuous Screamin' Eagle script will usually occupy a prominent location on the Harley-Davidson product. (For more information on Screamin' Eagle exhausts, see pages 54–55.)

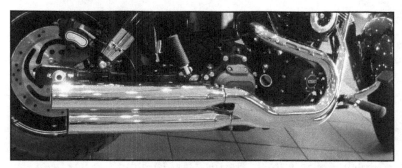

Figure 53. Dyna Fat Bob (Tommy Gun Exhaust, 2-1-2; no tapering at the end).

Figure 54. Dyna Wide Glide (Tommy Gun Exhaust, 2-1-2; no tapering at the end).

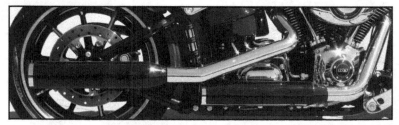

Figure 55. Softail Breakout (no tapering at the end).

Figure 56. Softail Slim (shown in photo), Softail Cross Bones, and Softail Blackline (no tapering at the end).

Unusual-looking Exhaust Systems Produced by Harley-Davidson

The Harley-Davidson Motor Company has also produced a few exhausts which are reminiscent of the exhaust systems commonly installed on sport bikes. These exhausts represent the exception in their product line, but it is important for law enforcement to know the appearance of these unusual-looking exhausts to avoid confusion, assuming they are examples of modified exhaust systems. Photographs of the exhausts for the Sportster XR 1200 and the Night Rod and Street Rod are available on TotalMotorcycle.com. Photographs of the Night Rod Special, the V-Rod, and the V-Rod Muscle are pictured below.

Figure 57. Night Rod Special (resembles sport bike exhaust).

Figure 58. V-Rod exhaust (unusual Harley-Davidson exhaust resembles sport bike exhaust).

Unlike Harley's touring models, which always have the exhaust on both sides of the motorcycle, it is important to realize that the exhaust systems on Harley-Davidson's Sportsters, Dynas, Softails, and V-Rods are *almost always* on the right side of the motorcycle. The rare exceptions include the V-Rod Muscle (pictured below), plus the Springer Softail Classic, the Springer Softail, and the Heritage Springer. One will find photographs of the last three older models on TotalMotorcycle.com.

Figure 59. V-Rod Muscle (unusual Harley-Davidson exhaust; present on right and left side of motorcycle).

The Importance of a 2-into-1 Exhaust on Harley-Davidson Motorcycles

A 2-into-1 exhaust refers to the merging of the two exhaust headers into a single exhaust; this arrangement is commonly seen with modified exhaust systems. However, this is not true for Harley-Davidson models, as stock 2-into-1 exhaust systems are rather uncommon.

Harley-Davidson has made only two basic styles of a 2-into-1 exhaust since 2007. One style occurs on their Dyna Switchback and the newer Low Rider model, along with the 2010 Street Glide and 2010 Road Glide Custom. The other style of their 2-into-1 exhaust is now installed on the new Street 500 and Street 750 models. If one learns the appearance of these two styles of Harley-Davidson's street-legal, 2-into-1 exhaust systems, the non-EPA-compliant 2-into-1 exhausts will become extremely conspicuous at considerable distance. Examples of Harley-Davidson's 2-into-1 exhaust systems are pictured below.

Figure 60. Dyna Switchback; Harley-Davidson's
unique 2-into-1 exhaust.

Figure 61. Harley-Davidson's 2015 Dyna Low Rider.
This 2-into-1 exhaust has the same configuration
as the Dyna Switchback pictured above.

Figure 62. Harley-Davidson's other configuration of a
2-into-1 exhaust featured on their Street 500 and
Street 750, which were introduced in 2015.

As mentioned above, examples of 2-into-1 exhaust systems are relatively uncommon on stock Harley-Davidson motorcycles. This is not true for the after-market modified exhaust systems. Note the different configuration of these 2-into-1 modified exhaust systems, all of which are installed on Harley-Davidson motorcycles.

**Figure 63. Harley-Davidson Dyna model
with modified 2-into-1 exhaust.**

**Figure 64. 2006 Harley-Davidson CVO Fat Boy with
modified 2-into-1 exhaust by Vance & Hines.**

Figure 65. Harley-Davidson V-Rod (Night Rod Special) with modified 2-into-1 exhaust by Vance & Hines.

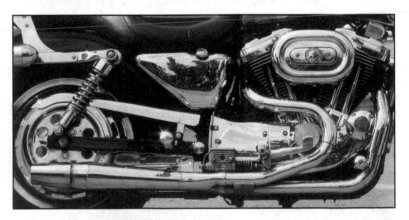

Figure 66. Harley-Davidson Sportster with modified 2-into-1 "Thunderheader" exhaust.

Figure 67. Harley-Davidson Road King touring
model with modified 2-into-1 exhaust.

Figure 68. Harley-Davidson model with
modified 2-into-1 exhaust.

Figure 69. Highly customized Harley-Davidson
model with modified 2-into-1 exhaust.

Typical Arrangement of Harley-Davidson's Exhaust Headers on Touring Models

Another feature worth learning with regard to Harley-Davidson touring models is the configuration and design of the exhaust headers. There have been only two configurations of the exhaust headers made by Harley-Davidson since EPA regulations went into effect in 1983. If the officer is aware of this fact, and is aware of the appearance of the two stock configurations, identification of a non-stock arrangement will be easy.

From the beginning of EPA regulations in 1983 through 2008, the standard arrangement of the exhaust headers for all Harley-Davidson touring models had the same configuration and appearance. Then, beginning in 2009, the company came out with an entirely new design, with their unique 2-into-1-into-2 arrangement of the exhaust system. Both configurations are pictured below.

Figure 70. Arrangement of exhaust headers for all Harley-Davidson touring models dating before the beginning of EPA regulations in 1983 through 2008; it is referred to as their "crossover duel exhaust."

Figure 71. Arrangement of exhaust headers for all Harley-Davidson touring models from the beginning of 2009 to present; it is referred to as a "2-into-1-into-2 exhaust."

To the contrary, the exhaust systems pictured below do not exhibit the typical arrangement of exhaust headers installed on Harley-Davidson motorcycles at the factory. Many of these modified exhaust systems are recognizable at considerable distance if one is aware of Harley-Davidson's stock appearance.

Figure 72. The arrangement of the exhaust headers made by Vance & Hines clearly deviates from any Harley-Davidson arrangement of exhaust headers. This Vance & Hines arrangement is perhaps the easiest one to identify by sight alone.

Figure 73. The arrangement of the exhaust headers made by Rinehart Racing also clearly deviates from any Harley-Davidson arrangement of exhaust headers. This is another example of an arrangement of the exhaust headers which is easy to identify by sight alone.

Figure 74. This "2-into-2" is another common arrangement of the exhaust headers on Harley-Davidson touring motorcycles. This is a sure indication of a modified exhaust system.

Figure 75. This "2-into-2 configuration" of exhaust headers installed on a Harley-Davidson touring model departs from either of Harley-Davidson's standard arrangements of stock exhaust headers (compare with Figures 70 and 71). A Vance & Hines logo appears on this exhaust.

Modified Exhaust Systems Which Mimic the Appearance of Stock

This group of modified exhaust systems will undoubtedly require inspecting for the EPA label to verify the EPA information (*or lack thereof, which will frequently be the case*) on the underneath side or perhaps the inboard side of these mufflers. If they lack a company logo they are particularly difficult to identify by sight alone.

Even though these exhaust systems may look like stock, they will sound conspicuously louder than stock. Hence, the ones that mimic the appearance of stock will be very conspicuous to the experienced officer (even at low rpm), just by sound alone. However, if verifiable, objective evidence is sought, the officer or vehicle inspector will need to locate the required EPA information stamped on the body of the muffler. It may require the use of a mirror to locate the EPA label, which is often located on the underneath side of the expansion chamber on Harley-Davidson models. Two examples of the EPA label are pictured below.

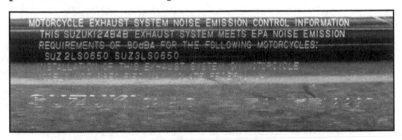

Figure 76. Representative example of an EPA label on the body of a muffler installed at the factory by Suzuki. This label states this muffler "meets EPA noise emission requirements" for the specific model in question.

Figure 77. Representative example of an EPA label on the body of a muffler installed at the factory by Harley-Davidson. The label states this muffler "meets EPA noise emission requirements" for the specific model in question.

Again, if the officer or vehicle inspector is actually dealing with one of the non-compliant exhaust systems, there is a very good chance that there will be no EPA information whatsoever located on the exhaust system. In the absence of EPA information, the offending exhaust will by default be a modified exhaust system—for the simple reason that all EPA-compliant exhausts are stamped at the factory.

An officer or inspector also has the potential to encounter a factory-installed exhaust, which should be EPA-approved, but exhibits excessive and unusual noise nonetheless. If this is the case, the potential always exists where the owner physically altered, damaged, or otherwise compromised the sound-deadening capabilities of the factory-installed exhaust. To examine for this type of tampering, inspection of the exhaust may become necessary. This may require the expertise of a professional motorcycle mechanic.

Figure 78. Modified exhaust by Python mimicking the appearance of stock exhaust installed on Harley-Davidson Softail model.

Figure 79. Modified exhaust by Vance & Hines mimicking the appearance of stock on this Harley-Davidson V-Rod Muscle (compare with exhaust in Figure 59).

3

EPA-Compliant After-Market Exhaust Systems

Only a tiny fraction of after-market exhaust systems meet strict EPA guidelines for noise emissions. These exhaust systems would be equivalent replacements for original factory-installed equipment. We are aware of only five such companies offering this type of product for Harley-Davidson motorcycles and the sport bike industry: Vance & Hines, BUB Enterprises, S&S, Akrapovic, and Yoshimura.

If the officer or inspector issues a citation based on the incorrect identification of a modified exhaust system, the owner can always challenge this citation. If the owner of the motorcycle was also the one who originally installed the factory-equivalent system, the owner will undoubtedly be very aware of this fact (given the expense and relative scarcity of these products). In fact, it requires a concentrated effort just to locate an after-market, factory-equivalent exhaust. If this occurs, the motorist will almost certainly assist the officer in locating the appropriate EPA information displayed on the exhaust. In this scenario, the EPA information will be the best friend a biker ever had.

HARLEY-DAVIDSON'S OWN BRAND OF EPA-COMPLIANT AFTER-MARKET EXHAUST

For EPA-compliant after-market exhaust systems capable of fitting *all models* of Harley-Davidson motorcycles, there is *only a single option*: Harley-Davidson's own Screamin' Eagle series of after-market exhausts. However, it is important to remember that Harley-Davidson made the conversion of their Screamin' Eagle exhausts from non-EPA-compliant to EPA-compliant in 2006. Many of these older non-EPA-compliant Screamin' Eagle exhausts are still in use in today. Although Harley-Davidson places the Screamin' Ealge script in a conspicuous location on the body of the muffler, in most instances the only way to know for certain whether the exhaust is EPA certified is to inspect for the EPA label on the underneath surface of the muffler. However, if the script on the body of the muffler reads, "Screamin' Eagle II," then one knows for certain it is one of the older, non-EPA-certified exhausts.

It is also important to note some of Harley-Davidson's after-market exhausts display the words "Harley-Davidson" in a conspicuous location on the expansion chamber instead of the words "Screamin' Eagle."

Representative photographs of Screamin' Eagle exhausts, along with the Screamin' Eagle script or the "Harley-Davidson" script, appear below.

Figure 80. Screamin' Eagle script on after-market
exhaust made by Harley-Davidson.

Figure 81. Screamin' Eagle script on after-market
exhaust by Harley-Davidson.

Figure 82. Screamin' Eagle II script displaying the logo
appearing on one of the older non-EPA-certified exhausts.
This muffler predates 2007.

Figure 83. "Harley-Davidson" script on after-market exhaust by Harley-Davidson.

COMPANIES OTHER THAN HARLEY-DAVIDSON OFFERING AN EPA-COMPLIANT EXHAUST FOR HARLEY-DAVIDSON MOTORCYCLES

We know of only three other companies offering EPA-compliant, after-market products that are compatible with Harley-Davidson motorcycles: Vance & Hines (Twin Slash Slip-ons), BUB Enterprises ("BUB 7 Cat," "BUB 7 Stealth," and "BUB Straight 8 Stealth Muffler"), and the S&S Company (80 dB SPO muffler). Importantly, the EPA-compliant exhausts made by these three companies are only compatible with Harley-Davidson's touring models, which means they are not compatible with Harley-Davidson's Softails, Dynas, Sportsters, and V-Rods.

Unfortunately, the physical appearance of these exhausts is not unique, as the after-market companies making these exhaust systems also make a non-EPA-compliant version, which cannot be safely separated by sight alone.

Even so, the officer may encounter examples of EPA-compliant, after-market exhausts (although the likelihood of this actually occurring is very remote). Again, in the case of the Vance & Hines product (regarding their *single*, EPA-compliant option), the appropriate EPA information is conveniently and conspicuously located on the *topside* of the expansion chamber. Thus, no mirror is required to visually inspect the EPA information for the Vance & Hines product. The Vance & Hines factory-equivalent exhaust is referred to as their "Twin Slash Slip-ons."

EPA-COMPLIANT AFTER-MARKET EXHAUST FOR THE SPORT BIKE INDUSTRY

The Yoshimura Company and the Akrapovic Company are the only two we know which make an EPA-compliant exhaust for sport bikes. Yoshimura offers the most options with five basic body styles. The EPA-compliant exhaust made by the Akrapovic Company is virtually identical to Yoshimura's R-77 model. None of these EPA-compliant after-market mufflers can be safely identified by sight alone. One must inspect for the EPA information (or lack thereof) on the body of the muffler.

4

Modified Exhaust Systems for Automobiles and Light Trucks

The use of "performance exhaust systems" in automobiles and light trucks is increasingly popular. These exhaust systems are not equivalent to those installed at the factory. They are designed to enhance power performance and thus increase noise emissions. For those states and municipalities which specifically prohibit the use of modified exhaust systems, performance exhaust systems are not legal for use on public roadways.

Unfortunately, there are no federal regulations governing exhaust noise emissions for automobiles and light trucks (as there are with motorcycles). Federal regulations are long overdue.

There is an obvious, fundamental difference between modified exhaust systems installed on motorcycles versus those on automobiles and light trucks. Since the exhaust systems on cars and trucks are essentially hidden from view, law enforcement officers and vehicle inspectors will not always be able to rely solely on visual appearance to identify these modified exhaust systems.

However, since most automobiles and light trucks operating on public roadways are factory-equipped with very effective exhaust systems and mufflers (and thus emit small amounts of exhaust noise), those equipped with modified exhaust systems are conspicuously noisy. By this simple observation, police officers or vehicle inspectors can identify suspect vehicles and issue citations.

We have provided a list of popular brands of "performance" exhaust systems, along with the product descriptions found on their web sites. Those product descriptions leave little doubt that those modified exhaust systems create far more noise than factory-installed equipment. Many of those products are labeled with their manufacturer's logo (making it very easy for inspection mechanics to identify them).

Borla exhaust: "aggressive."

BBK Varitune performance mufflers: "8-10 Decibel sound Range Adjustment."

FlowTech afterburner mufflers: "Awesome sound."

FlowTech Purple Hornies glasspack muffler: "Classic muscle car sound."

AFE scorpion mufflers: "Baffled design for aggressive sound."

Hooker mufflers: "Produce an aggressive, muscle car sound."

FlowMaster Delta Flow: "Deep, aggressive, high-performance exhaust note."

Banks Monster muffler: "Rich, Throaty Sound."

Thrush exhaust: "Deep, muscle-car tone."

Cherry Bomb glass pack mufflers: "Disturbing the Peace Since 1968."

SLP Loud Mouth Resonators: "Switch between muffled and wide open."

"MagnaFlow is proud to announce its new cat-back exhaust for the Ford Mustang Shelby GT350. MagnaFlow brings an aggressive sound to help unlock its full potential."

Conclusion

Noise pollution is a significant national problem. Excessive noise threatens public health and degrades the quality of life.

Motorists do not have the right to illegally tamper with their vehicle's exhaust system. They do not have the right to assault the public with invasive noise two to four times that allowed by federal law. This acoustical problem has been unchecked for far too long.

We know of no municipality or state which has adequately brought this problem under control. Clearly, it is time to consider a new approach. We at Noise Free America: A Coalition to Promote Quiet are now offering that new approach.

We believe this primarily sight-based method for identifying modified exhaust systems, combined with a shift in focus away from the symptoms of the problem (excessive and unusual noise) to an approach addressing the root cause of the problem (illegal modifications to the exhaust system) is the best option available.

Traditional methods used to address this problem have been a profound and dismal failure. It is time to consider the fresh, new approach presented in this guide.

Appendix A: Guidance for Prosecutors

The purpose of this appendix is to provide information which can assist in the prosecution of cases involving excessive motor vehicle exhaust noise and improper exhaust systems.

To effectively mitigate the problem of excessively loud motor vehicles, relevant laws must be proactively enforced—rather than relying solely on citizen complaints.

The enforcement must be carefully crafted and not rely solely on exhaust noise testing with decibel meters (which has proven far too cumbersome, technically inadequate, and ineffective).

The enforcement process should include the use of the simple-to-enforce "excessive or unusual noise" criterion, along with an inspection element to identify the root cause of excessive motor vehicles exhaust noise: modified exhaust systems.

There are three steps in dealing with the problem of excessively loud vehicles: (a) establishing appropriate laws and enforcement policies; (b) enforcing the policy; and (c) adjudicating the charge in court.

Police enforcement entails (a) observing the violation; (b) stopping the offending vehicle; (c) citing the operator with the appropriate charge; and (d) testifying in court.

THE "EXCESSIVE OR UNUSUAL NOISE" ENFORCEMENT CRITERION

"Excessive or unusual noise" is the enforcement criterion employed by most police officers when enforcing motor vehicle noise and muffler laws. The motor vehicle exhaust noise and muffler laws of practically all 50 states have one key phrase in common: "excessive or unusual noise."

For example, the Virginia muffler law states, "Every motor vehicle subject to registration shall at all times be equipped with an adequate muffler in constant operation and properly maintained to prevent any *excessive or unusual noise*, and no muffler or exhaust system shall be equipped with a cutout, bypass, or similar device."

According to the Delaware muffler law, "No person shall drive a motor vehicle, including a motorcycle, on a highway, including residential streets, unless such motor vehicle or motorcycle is equipped with a muffler in good working order and in accordance with manufacturer's specifications and in constant operation to prevent *excessive or unusual noise*."

The muffler law of North Carolina states, "No person shall drive a motor vehicle on a highway unless such motor vehicle is equipped with a muffler, or other exhaust system of the type installed at the time of manufacture, in good working order and in constant operation to prevent *excessive or unusual noise.*"

The phrase "excessive or unusual noise" has been upheld by the courts as being both objective and constitutional. Any police officer can enforce this standard without any sound measuring equipment. These muffler laws also recognize the root cause of "excessive and unusual" noise; therefore, they require factory-equivalent mufflers.

Using the standard of "excessive or unusual noise," the exhaust noise emissions of motor vehicles with altered exhaust systems are very evident. Police officers should not hesitate to employ this very simple enforcement method; in addition, prosecutors and courts should recognize its validity.

The simple observation of "excessive and unusual noise" emanating from the exhaust systems of motor vehicles provides valid probable cause to stop and ticket the operators of those motor vehicles.

However, offenders ticketed for "excessive and unusual noise" will sometimes challenge this criterion as being subjective and unconstitutionally vague. Appellate courts have upheld that criterion for assessing excessive exhaust noise. However, some lower courts have erroneously viewed this criterion as unconstitutionally vague. This outcome is worsened by poorly-written laws which do not instruct the courts to accept the testimony of police officers that the noise was "excessive and unusual."

When prosecutors are faced with such a challenge, they should rebut it with the case law presented here.

Case Law Upholding The "Excessive And Unusual Noise" Criterion

In *Smith v. Peterson*, the California Court of Appeals reversed a trial court ruling that the phrase "excessive or unusual noise" used in the state exhaust noise and muffler law was unconstitutionally vague. *Smith v. Peterson* has been cited in many similar cases by courts in other states.

Smith v. Peterson, California Court of Appeals. Fourth Dist., Mar. 2, 1955.131 Cal.App.2d 241, 249-50, 280 P.2d 522 (1955):

> "It appears to us that the requirement that a motor vehicle be equipped with a muffler in constant operation so as to prevent any excessive or unusual noise seems as certain as any rule which could be practically enforced.
>
> Motor vehicles have been used so long and have become so common, and mufflers so uniformly used to minimize the noise from their exhaust that what is usual has become a matter of common knowledge, and anything in excess of that is excessive and unusual, and usually capable of ascertainment as such.
>
> We conclude that the words 'excessive' or 'unusual,' when viewed in the context in which they are used, are sufficiently certain to inform persons of ordinary intelligence of the nature of the offense which is prohibited, and are therefore sufficient to establish a standard of

conduct which is ascertainable by persons familiar with the operation of automobiles."

In *State of North Dakota v. Robin S. Beyer*, the North Dakota Supreme Court rejected the argument that *"the language of Section 39-21-37, N.D.C.C., requiring all vehicles to be equipped with a muffler in good working order to prevent "excessive or unusual noise," is "too broad and subject to too many interpretations to be fairly administrated."*

The court cited *Smith v. Peterson* and stated: *"Our research reveals a line of cases from other jurisdictions which has rejected vagueness challenges to statutes substantively identical to Section 39-21-37, N.D.C.C., requiring vehicles to be equipped with mufflers to prevent 'excessive or unusual noise.' We have found no cases concluding that this statutory language is unconstitutionally vague or indefinite, and neither the parties nor the county court have cited such a case."*

In upholding a similar California statutory provision, the California District Court of Appeals for the Fourth District concluded that "the words 'excessive' or 'unusual,' when viewed in the context in which they are used are sufficiently certain to inform persons of ordinary intelligence of the nature of the offense which is prohibited, and are therefore sufficient to establish a standard of conduct which is ascertainable by persons familiar with the operation of automobiles." Smith v. Peterson, supra, 280 P.2d at 528.

The meaning of "excessive" and "unusual" is well within the common understanding of not only drivers, but also police offi-

cers. To adjudge excessive or unusual noise, officers must rely on their sense of hearing, just as they must rely on their sense of sight for speeding violations or their sense of smell for DUI violations.

In *State v. Cobbs*, the Florida District Court of Appeals concluded: "*a police officer, who determined through his own sense of hearing that the defendant's motorcycle made 'excessive or unusual' noise, had an articulable suspicion justifying the officer's stop of the defendant.*" In so concluding, the court stated:

> "A police officer's hearing may deceive him, but so may his sense of sight, smell, taste, and touch. We do not require that an officer's suspicion prove to be right; we require only that the suspicion be founded and articulable. Moreover, the law does not require that every police officer have with him a narcotics-sniffing dog, a panoramic breathalyzer, a radar gun, or a decibel counter to verify what he smells or sees or hears.
>
> The defendant argues that to sanction a stop without absolute certainty that the statutory noise limit was exceeded is fraught with potential for abuse. We see no greater potential for abuse in this case than in any case where an officer's visual observations of a vehicle's progress lead him to the founded suspicion that the driver of a vehicle is committing a traffic offense. . . . So long as there exists a basis from which courts can determine that the stop was not arbitrary . . . the fact that that basis

comes from an officer's testimony about what his senses revealed does not make the stop any less justified.

An officer's observations based upon his sense of hearing are subject to the same type of trial scrutiny, through cross examination and introduction of rebuttal evidence, as are all other observations made by an officer. We conclude that the phrase 'excessive or unusual noise' provides sufficient guidelines to govern law enforcement officers."

For many years, case law at the appellate level has upheld the "excessive and unusual noise" criterion adopted by most, if not all, state motor vehicles codes and countless county and municipal motor vehicle noise ordinances.

We now address another important element of the adjudication process: inspections.

THE INSPECTION ELEMENT

Some lower courts have accepted challenges to the reliability of the police officer's observations of the excessive or unusual noise emitted by the defendant's vehicle. The defendant may also claim the vehicle's exhaust system and muffler is legal under state law and promise to operate the vehicle quietly in the future. Such defenses should not be accepted by the courts. Doing so would mean that the defendants' noisy modified exhaust systems would still be in place.

The root cause of excessive motor vehicle exhaust noise is not how motor vehicles are *operated*. Rather, the root cause is how motor vehicles are *equipped*. Excessive motor vehicle noise is caused by the illicit tampering with, or modification of, motor vehicle exhaust systems and by the use of after-market exhaust systems and mufflers that are not factory-equivalent or as effective in preventing excessive or unusual noise as those originally installed at the time of manufacture.

The penalty for violating vehicle exhaust and muffler laws is often a simple fine. That is not a sufficient remedy, as it allows the vehicle to continue to blast away on public roads and highways.

THE INSPECTION ELEMENT PROVIDES ADDITIONAL SUPPORTING EVIDENCE

This guide presents a motor vehicle noise control concept based on exhaust system equipment standards. It presents an alternative method of approaching motor vehicle noise control and enforcement. Our suggested approach augments the evidence of not only an exhaust noise emission violation, but of an exhaust equipment violation as well; this provides prosecutors with additional objective supporting evidence. Offenders should not only be ticketed for "excessive and unusual noise," but also for an equipment violation. Such improper equipment is the root cause of the "excessive and unusual noise."

To provide that additional objective supporting evidence for effectively prosecuting these cases, an inspection of the exhaust system and muffler of the defendant's vehicle should be performed. The purpose of the inspection is to determine if the vehicle is equipped with a non-factory equivalent exhaust system.

Such inspections may be carried out by police officers in the field. However, not all police officers may feel comfortable performing exhaust system inspections, even for motorcycles—in spite of the fact that a vehicle's exhaust systems are in the open and easy to access. The exhaust systems of cars and light trucks, being beneath the vehicles, are not easily accessible by police officers in the field; thus, they may require the services of a state-certified motor vehicle mechanic.

THE BEST REMEDY FOR MITIGATING THE PROBLEM

Merely fining the operator of the vehicle for operating a vehicle that emits excessive or unusual noise without mitigating the root cause of that noise is not a sufficient remedy. If an inspection reveals that the exhaust system has been illegally modified, the owner of the vehicle should be required to have that equipment violation corrected to bring the vehicle into compliance with the state muffler law. Any highway motor vehicle which is not equipped in compliance with the state motor vehicle code is not eligible to be registered for operating on public highways.

In order to implement the process recommended by this appendix, it may be necessary to revise state motor vehicle codes and/or municipal laws. That is the subject of "Appendix B: Guidance for Legislators."

Appendix B: Guidance for Legislators

This section provides guidance for crafting laws that more effectively address excessive motor vehicle noise and improper mufflers.

To implement the process suggested by this appendix, state law should be amended to make it clear to the courts and law enforcement officers that the observation of "excessive or unusual noise" is reasonable grounds for a police officer stopping a vehicle and/or issuing a citation. Additional reasonable grounds include observing prohibited equipment or signs of tampering. State law should also specify that no sound testing shall be required to enforce the provisions of the law.

Some states require annual or biannual motor vehicle safety inspections, but many states have eliminated those inspections. States which retain safety inspections are at an advantage, since regular, mandatory motor vehicle inspections can detect unlawfully modified exhaust systems and improper mufflers. Carrying out regular inspections can greatly lessen the enforcement burden on the police and better protect the public from excessively loud motor vehicles.

STATES WITHOUT REGULAR SAFETY INSPECTIONS

In states without regular safety inspections, we recommend the following:

(A) Implement an inspection process which enlists the aid of motor vehicle mechanics for inspecting the exhaust systems of vehicles for enforcing the state exhaust system equipment requirements. The inspection process shall incorporate the elements in the suggested legislative language.

(B) The mandatory inspection shall be triggered by a motorist cited for violating the state motor vehicle noise emissions and muffler law. The inspection mechanics shall be provided with a detailed inspection procedure incorporating the elements in the suggested legislative language. The results of the inspection shall be provided to the citing officer and the prosecutor as evidence of an exhaust system equipment violation.

STATES WITH REGULAR SAFETY INSPECTIONS

In states with regular safety inspections, we recommend the following:

(A) Amend the current safety inspection process to incorporate the elements in the suggested legislative language and provide inspection mechanics with a detailed inspection procedure based on it.

(B) Establish a mandatory inspection triggered whenever a motorist is cited for violating the state motor vehicle noise emissions and muffler law, utilizing state-certified mechanics. The inspection mechanics shall be provided with a detailed inspection procedure, incorporating the elements in the suggested legislative language. The results of the inspection shall be provided to the citing officer and the prosecutor as evidence of an exhaust system equipment violation.

BURDEN OF PROOF STANDARD: PREPONDERANCE OF EVIDENCE

Some states use the "beyond a reasonable doubt" standard for an exhaust system infraction. That standard of proof is not appropriate for motor vehicle noise and equipment infractions. That standard is more appropriate for misdemeanors and felonies, which (unlike motor vehicle noise and equipment infractions) carry jail time. Prosecutors often dismiss vehicle noise cases because of a mistaken belief that meeting the "beyond a reasonable doubt" standard requires the use of decibel meters. That process is much too cumbersome, technically inadequate, and enforcement-inhibiting, and does not deal with the root cause of the problem.

Some states use the "preponderance of evidence" burden of proof for motor vehicle infractions. This standard is far less burdensome for the state and much more appropriate for enforcing motor vehicle noise and equipment infractions. State codes should apply the "preponderance of evidence" burden of proof to motor vehicle infractions.

Suggested Language for Revising the State Motor Vehicle Exhaust Noise and Muffler Law

We suggest that states adopt the following language for their law regulating state motor vehicle noise and exhausts:

No person shall drive any motor vehicle on a highway and no motor vehicle shall be registered for highway use and no motor vehicle registered in the state shall pass the state's annual motor vehicle safety inspection unless such motor vehicle is equipped with a muffler, or exhaust system, or noise emission control device, that is of the type installed at the time of manufacture, in good working order and in constant operation to prevent excessive or unusual noise, plainly visible smoke and smoke screens, or is not equipped with an exhaust system that complies with the following four elements of this section, or is equipped with an exhaust system of the types prohibited by element (5) of this section. And it shall be unlawful to use a "muffler cut-out" on any motor vehicle upon a highway.

(1) The muffler, if not original equipment, must reduce exhaust noise levels to that of the vehicle's original equipment and shall comply with any federal and state regulatory requirements which may apply. No person shall alter or make additions to a vehicle's muffler or any other part of the vehicle or its noise emission control devices such as to cause the vehicle's noise emissions to exceed that as origi-

nally manufactured or render it out of compliance with any federal and state regulatory requirements that may apply.

(2) No person shall modify the exhaust system or engine or noise control devices of any motor vehicle in a manner that will or may amplify or noticeably increase the noise emitted by the engine of such vehicle or by the exhaust system as originally installed on the vehicle, and it shall be unlawful for any person to register or operate a motor vehicle on public highways that is not equipped as required by this section, or which has been modified in a manner prohibited by state law.

(3) All highway and off-road use motorcycles operated in the state manufactured after December 31, 1982, shall be equipped as required by federal regulation CFR 40, part 205, sub parts D & E, pursuant to the federal Noise Control Act of 1972, to include a labeled EPA-compliant exhaust system specific to the make and model indicating compliance with federal noise emission limits, free of defects or modifications. Nothing in this section shall prevent the installation of any properly certified, labeled, and unaltered with the exception of mounting hardware, EPA-compliant replacement mufflers on motorcycles.

(4) Every highway and off-road use motorcycle, regardless of model year, shall be equipped with a factory equivalent muffler designed for that class of motorcycle and of the type installed at the time of manufacture, free of defects and modifications, in good working order and in constant operation and that prevents the escape of excessive or unusual noise as assessed by the plainly audible criterion.

The muffler, if not original equipment, must reduce exhaust noise levels to that of the vehicle's original equipment.

(5) Prohibited exhaust system equipment and modifications:

(a) No highway motor vehicle shall be equipped with a straight pipe exhaust system or chambered pipes regardless of the presence of baffles, or a hollow core muffler, or "glass-pack" or a "performance muffler" or "sport muffler" that does not by the manufacturers certification affidavit maintain exhaust noise emissions to no greater than, and that is indistinguishable from, that emitted by the original factory installed exhaust system or has not provided documented assurance that the product complies with the requirements of this subsection and with elements 1, 2, 3, and 4 of this section, or by the manufacturer's admission or advertisement noticeably alters or noticeably increases exhaust noise emissions of a vehicle it is used on as compared to the original factory installed exhaust system, or does not comply with any federal regulations that may apply.

No highway motor vehicle shall be equipped with a muffler that is labeled for "off road use," or is labeled as or marketed for "closed course competition use only," or for "use on closed courses only," or if not labeled can be shown to be intended for "off road use," or for "closed course competition use only," or for "use on closed courses only," or a "muffler cut-out, " bypass, or similar device, or exhaust system with removable baffles, removable or adjustable noise suppression elements or devices, or whistle tips or similar devices.

(b) No off-road motorcycle manufactured since December 31, 1982 shall be equipped with any equipment prohibited by this sub-section, with the exception of properly labeled and unaltered EPA-compliant off-road mufflers manufactured for use on off-road motorcycles of its type and engine displacement or horsepower.

(c) No person shall remove, obscure, or deface, or counterfeit any label of compliance or mark required by federal law or state law which is affixed to any motor vehicle or motor vehicle part for purposes of identifying the motor vehicle or motor vehicle part as a federally or state regulated product or its intended use. No person shall allow any label of compliance or mark to be removed or rendered obscured, defaced, or unreadable.

(d) No person shall sell, or offer for sale, or install, or allow to be installed, for use on any highway or off-road motor vehicle, any exhaust system which is not of the type meeting the requirements of state law, or is of the types prohibited by state law.

Definitions:

(1) The term "section" refers to state motor vehicle exhaust noise and muffler law.

(2) The term "exhaust system" means the combination of components, including mufflers and other sound dissipative devices, which provides for the enclosed flow of exhaust gas from the engine exhaust port to the atmosphere. "Exhaust system" further means any constituent components of the combination which conduct exhaust gases and which are sold as separate products. "Exhaust system" does not mean any of the constituent components of the combination, alone, which do not conduct exhaust gases, such as brackets and other mounting hardware.

(3) The term "muffler" is defined as a device consisting of a series of chambers and baffle plates, for the purpose of receiving exhaust gas from an internal combustion engine, and is effective in reducing engine exhaust noise emissions.

(4) The term "hollow core muffler" (also known as a "straight-through muffler") is a type of muffler where the exhaust inlet is visible from the exhaust outlet, whereby exhaust gases pass straight through the center of the muffler.

(5) The term "glasspack" is defined as is a type of hollow core muffler in which the exhaust gas passes straight through the center of the muffler where fiberglass, or other material, surrounds the exhaust channel to absorb some of the exhaust sound.

(6) The term "OEM" means "original equipment manufacture," and refers to original equipment or replacement part supplied by the original manufacture of a motor vehicle.

(7) The term "for use on closed courses only" means any motor vehicle or component designed and marketed, or designated by regulation, as solely for use only in closed course competition events and not legal for use on public highways or on highway vehicles, and for motorcycles does not comply with federal regulations pertaining to highway and off-road motorcycles as per 40 CFR 205, parts D & E.

(8) The term "off-road motorcycle" means any motorcycle that is not a street or highway motorcycle or competition motorcycle.

(9) The term "noise emission control system" means any motor vehicle part, component or system, the purpose of which includes control or the reduction noise emitted from a vehicle, including all exhaust system components.

(10) The term "excessive or unusual" is defined as noise emitted by a motor vehicle that is noticeably louder, or of a quality noticeably uncharacteristic or atypical of the vehicle as originally manufactured or that of similar vehicles operating in the environment, and for the purposes of enforcing this section, may be assessed by the plainly audible criterion.

(11) The term "plainly audible" is defined as any sound which can be detected by a reasonable person of unimpaired auditory senses using his or her unaided hearing faculties.

(12) The term "excessive noise" is defined as noise levels noticeably in excess of that emitted by unaltered and properly functioning vehicles as originally manufactured and not blending in with the noise emissions of vehicles operating in the vicinity. The standard of comparison by which excessive noise is assessed by the plainly audible criteria is the noise emissions of the vehicle as originally manufactured and in comparison to similar legally equipped vehicles.

(13) The term "unusual noise" is defined as any quality in noise emissions that is noticeably unusual or not typical of a legally equipped and unaltered motor vehicle of its particular class and as originally manufactured. The observation of "excessive or unusual noise" by law enforcement officers by the plainly

audible criterion is probable cause in initiating a stop and in enforcing this section. Such unusual qualities are unusual humming, buzzing, rumbling, roaring, growling, popping, or jack hammer-like exhaust noise emissions not typical of properly equipped and maintained highway vehicles and that which does not blend in with the noise emissions of vehicles operating in the vicinity. The standard of comparison by which unusual noise is assessed by the plainly audible criterion is the normal noise emissions of a legally-equipped and unaltered vehicle as originally manufactured.

(14) The term "whistle tips" is defined as a device that is applied to or is a modification of a motor vehicle's exhaust pipe that creates a high-pitched or shrieking noise when the motor vehicle is operated.

(15) The term "EPA-compliant" is defined as in compliance with federal regulation CFR 40, part 205, sub parts D & E, pursuant to the federal Noise Control Act of 1972.

Resources

TOTAL MOTORCYLE

- TotalMotorcycle.com

The best single resource showing the majority of all makes and models of motorcycles (many dating before 2000) in their stock condition as they would appear off the factory floor. This is an excellent resource for identifying the appearance of the factory-installed exhaust system.

DAVID B. TOREY AND JEFFREY R. MCCULLEY, "LIMITING MOTORCYCLE EXHAUST NOISE THROUGH AMENDMENT OF THE MOTOR VEHICLE CODE AND ITS REGULATIONS"

- *Temple Journal of Science, Technology, and Environmental Law*, spring 2006.
- Temple.edu/law/tjstel/2006/spring/v25no1-Torrey-and-McCulley.pdf

The authors propose amending Pennsylvania's motor vehicle code by incorporating federal manufacturing standards for motorcycle mufflers. It proposes requiring motorcycles to be equipped with EPA-approved mufflers and prohibiting various types of after-market exhaust systems and acts of tampering commonly employed by motorcyclists to make their motorcycles excessively loud. The authors' proposal simplifies the EPA's "label match-up" plan so that inspection mechanics and law enforcement personnel need only check for one label--that is, the label embossed on the muffler.

The *Guide to Modified Exhaust Systems* proposes a further simplification based on visually identifying motorcycle after-market mufflers and exhaust systems known not to be EPA-approved for use on all federally regulated motorcycles, many of which are not properly labeled (as required by federal law).

The *Guide to Modified Exhaust Systems* also provides guidance on how to visually identify improper modified exhaust systems sometimes used on pre-regulation motorcycles manufactured before December 31, 1982, the most common of which and troublesome are straight pipes.

NOISE FREE AMERICA: A COALITION TO PROMOTE QUIET

- NoiseFree.org

Contains extensive information on motorcycle noise.

Noise Off

- NoiseOff.org/motorcycles.php
- NoiseOff.org/pipes

Presents extensive material on the Noise Control Act of 1972 and the federal motorcycle noise emissions and mufflers regulations, 40 CFR 205 D&E. It also provides many references to relevant legislative findings, studies, regulatory and legal issues.

40 CFR 250 Parts D and E : Federal Motorcycle Noise Emissions and Muffler Regulations.

- ECFR.gov/cgi-bin/text-idx?tpl=/ecfrbrowse/Title40/40tab_02.tpl
- TITLE 40: Protection of Environment
- Sub-Chapter 6: Noise Abatement Programs
- Part 205 Sub-part D: Motorcycles
- Part 205 Sub-part E: Motorcycle Exhaust Systems

Sub-part E pertains to replacement motorcycle mufflers and is most relevant to the "Guide to Modified Exhaust Systems."

Glossary

after-market exhausts: Exhaust systems or mufflers manufactured and marketed for use on vehicles after the sale of the vehicle by the original equipment manufacturer to the consumer to replace original equipment parts.

chopper: A general term for a radically-modified factory made motorcycle or a custom-made motorcycle. These motorcycles characteristically have an extended front fork. The exhaust systems installed on choppers are almost never in compliance with EPA regulations or of the type that are factory installed on highway motorcycles. Choppers are commonly equipped with exhaust systems intended for use on closed courses only.

crossover dual exhaust: The term used by Harley-Davidson for the type of exhaust present on their touring models predating EPA regulations up until 2009. In 2009, Harley-Davidson began manufacturing a "2-into-1-into-2" exhaust on all their touring models. This 2-into-1-into-2 arrangement means the exhaust gases from the two header pipes merge into a common section of the exhaust system, and then separate again into two distinct tailpipes.

cruisers: A general term for a broad category of motorcycles, which are smaller and lighter than touring models, but heavier and slower than sport bikes. Although optional, saddlebags and fairings (windshields) are generally not present on cruisers, and they generally do not offer all of the deluxe features one would find on your typical touring model. More than any other category of motorcycles, cruisers probably have the highest percentage of modified exhaust systems. This is especially true with regard to the presence of straight pipes.

drag pipes: This term is synonymous with straight pipes. These exhaust systems often have absolutely no sound-deadening capabilities, and they have never been installed by a manufacturer for the intended use on public roadways. Their use was designed for closed courses only, even with the optional sound baffles installed.

end treatments: For the purpose of this guide, "end treatments" refer to any cosmetic (nonfunctional) addition to the very end of an exhaust system. They are for aesthetics only. "Shark tail" end treatments are perhaps the most common type of end treatment.

EPA-compliant: Descriptive of motorcycle exhaust systems—specifically, mufflers that have been manufactured and certified to be in compliance with the requirements of 40 CFR 205 parts D & E. Also sometimes referred to as "EPA-approved." In the case of motorcycle mufflers, it indicates that the muffler, when used on the motorcycle it is designed for, will effectively suppress exhaust noise emissions so as to maintain the motorcycle's total noise emissions within federal limits.

EPA label: The label of certification and compliance with the noise suppression performance requirements of 40 CFR 205 parts D& E embossed on motorcycle mufflers and which also indicates the intended use for the motorcycle muffler.

expansion chamber: A design feature of an effective muffler that allows for the expansion of exhaust gases before they exit the muffler and which aids in the suppression of exhaust noise. The outermost component or body of a muffler larger than the diameter of the exhaust pipes.

factory-installed exhaust systems: The exhaust system installed at the time of manufacture.

light trucks: A truck of maximum 8500 lb GVWR, Max 6000 lb curb weight, and Max 45 ft^2 frontal area. For example: pick-up trucks and SUVs.

modified exhaust system: An exhaust which is not factory-equivalent, does not comply with applicable federal regulatory standards, and is not suitable or legal for use on highway vehicles where modified exhaust systems are prohibited. This includes the physical tampering or alterations to an existing factory-installed exhaust system.

non-compliant exhausts: Exhaust systems which are not in compliance with EPA regulations, which took effect in 1983 for all motorcycles destined for the American market.

performance exhaust systems: An exhaust system designed to enhance power performance at the expense of exhaust noise suppression performance. Sometimes used to replace factory-installed exhaust systems and that often results in increased exhaust noise emissions.

sound baffles: A component of aftermarket motorcycle exhaust systems intended to restrict exhaust flow, are often a component of straight pipe exhaust systems, are often removable and are typically small and very ineffective devices that only minimally reduces exhaust noise emissions.

sport bikes: A general category of motorcycles designed and built for speed. They are lighter and much faster than touring bikes or cruisers. They frequently show a very stream-lined appearance. Both the bikes and the exhaust systems frequently display bright colors. Most are foreign-made.

stock condition: A general term for all parts and components of a vehicle (including the exhaust system), which would be present at the time of manufacture.

stock exhaust system: The type of exhaust system installed at the time of manufacture.

straight pipes: A motorcycle exhaust system that has the outward appearance of a uniform, consistent diameter the entire length of the system and does not possess an expansion chamber.

tampering: The unlawful modification of the regulated components of a motor vehicle either by altering factory installed components or by replacing regulated components with components that do not meet regulatory standards and are not factory equivalent.

tapering: Refers to a narrowing at the very end of an exhaust system. In most all instances, this is an indication of a factory-installed exhaust.

2-into-1 exhaust: Motorcycles which have two exhaust pipes emerging from the engine merge into a common exhaust pipe. This type of arrangement is much more common on modified exhaust systems (non-EPA-compliant) than it is on factory-installed exhaust systems.

2-into-2 exhaust: Motorcycles which have two exhaust pipes emerging from the engine, which results in two tailpipes.

touring models: Large, heavy motorcycles, which offer comfort and deluxe options as their primary selling feature. They are characterized by the presence of saddlebags and fairings (windshields), as their hallmark appearance.

Index

Noise Free America: A Coalition to Promote Quiet

Noise Free America: A Coalition to Promote Quiet is the nation's most prominent anti-noise organization, focusing on excessive noise from motorcycles, loud car stereos, and leaf blowers. Noise Free America: A Coalition to Promote Quiet has dozens of chapters in around 25 states. Members of Noise Free America: A Coalition to Promote Quiet conduct anti-noise public education campaigns at the local, state, and federal levels. The organization provides an "Ask an Expert" service, with advice to the public from a noise control engineer and a former Houston police officer.

Noise Free America: A Coalition to Promote Quiet issues a monthly "Noisy Dozen" press release, highlighting excessive noise in a community, business, or industry, or by an individual. Noise Free America: A Coalition to Promote Quiet has been featured in more than 350 media stories, including on *20/20*, CNN, and NPR, as well as in *Time* magazine, the *New York Times*, and the *Washington Post*. The organization's web site contains numerous noise ordinances, a model noise ordinance, radio public service announcements, sample letters, and a manual on "How to Fight Noise."

Noise Free America: A Coalition to Promote Quiet
NoiseFree.org
director@noisefree.org
877-664-7366
PO Box 2754
Chapel Hill, North Carolina 27515

SHARE THIS BOOK

If you find this book useful, share this information with your colleagues ...

Order additional copies of
Guide to Modified Exhaust Systems

Discounts available for law enforcement agencies and bulk purchases

Ask about a customized cover with your organization's logo, seal, motto, or message

To order, call
1-800-345-4447
or visit
www.quilldriverbooks.com/motorcycle

Comments or suggestions?

We welcome the advice of law enforcement in improving future editions of this book.

Send your comments to: info@quilldriverbooks.com

Printed in the USA
CPSIA information can be obtained
at www.ICGtesting.com
JSHW012011140824
68134JS00023B/2369

9 781610 353120